THE VOYAGE THAT CHANGED THE WORLD

Thekla Priebst

WIDE EYED EDITIONS

CONTENTS

INTRODUCTION

- 6 **A Rare and Precious Treasure**
- 8 **The Spice Trade**
- 10 **The Maritime Race for Spice**
- 12 **The Navigator's Gambit**

EUROPE

- 14 **Into the Unknown**
- 16 **The Sailors**
- 18 **One Mission, Many Languages**
- 20 **Sea of Rivalry**
- 22 **Guiding Lights**
- 24 **Becalmed and Betrayed**

SOUTH AMERICA

- 26 **Arrival in the Jungle Bay**
- 28 **Forbidden Paradise**
- 30 **Curious Exchanges**
- 32 **Frostbitten Hopes**
- 34 **Mutiny and Misfortune**
- 36 **An Inhumane Deceit**
- 38 **Storms and Saltwater**
- 40 **Lost in the Maze**
- 42 **Tears of Triumph**

OCEANIA

- 44 **The Wide Blue Yonder**
- 46 **Adrift in the Known Unknown**
- 48 **Desolate Seas**
- 50 **Shadows on the Shore**

SOUTH EAST ASIA

- 52 **Whispers of the Archipelago**
- 54 **Echoes of Conquest and Resistance**
- 56 **The Unyielding Shore**
- 58 **The Betrayal**
- 60 **A Leaderless Crew**
- 62 **The End of the Quest**
- 64 **Where the Clove Tree Grows**
- 66 **Divergent Paths**

AFRICA

- 68 **The Sole Stop**

EUROPE

- 70 **Triumph and Tragedy**
- 72 **Return of the Victoria**
- 74 **Beyond Cloves**
- 76 **The Legacy**

- 78 **Glossary**

A RARE AND PRECIOUS TREASURE

The Moluccas lie clustered at the point where the warm waters of the Indian Ocean meet the vast blue Pacific.

There, in the constant warmth and the healthy volcanic soil, grows a very special tree. Narrow and tall, it produces precious buds — but only after six or seven years.

At just the right time, and ever so carefully, these closed blooms are plucked by hand, then laid out to dry.

This is a tradition that the people who come from these islands have passed down, along with their history, from one generation to the next, through spoken stories.

Slowly, the buds dry and shrink, their stems turning from pale green to deep brown as they reveal their distinctive scent and taste – both sharp and sweet at the same time.

These little brown stems possess many powers. As well as giving a unique flavour to food, they can also preserve it. They have even been used in medicines and healing remedies.

They are known as cengkih. Cloves. And, like the islands they come from, they are small but mighty.

THE SPICE TRADE

This is a story that begins a very, very long time ago . . . so long ago that parts of the world remain uncharted by Europeans, who still call the Moluccas 'the Spice Islands'.

At this time, these islands are the only place in the world where cloves, nutmeg and mace grow. And of all these treasures, cloves are the most precious, because they can be found on only five small islands: Ternate, Tidore, Moti, Makian and Bacan.

The Spice Routes

The Spice Routes, also known as the Maritime Silk Roads, is a system of maritime trade routes spanning 15,000 kilometres, linking the East with the West. The sea routes ran from the coasts of East Asia, through the islands of Indonesia, around India to the Middle East, where they crossed the Mediterranean to reach the heart of Europe. The most important and most profitable goods traded were spices – hence the names of the routes.

It is estimated that as many as 500 plant species have been used as spices worldwide over the course of history. In Southeast Asia alone, there are 275 species. Spices were once in such demand that they influenced politics, economics and culture all over the world.

As well as trade, the Spice Routes brought together different ideas, concepts, knowledge and experiences from people of different nations.

The Spice Routes
in the 15th Century

Austronesian sailors are the first to take cloves to India, and for thousands of years cloves and other spices are freely traded by Greek, Roman, Arab, Persian, Indian, Javanese, Malay and Chinese merchants along natural trade routes that span half the globe.

To begin with, Europeans don't worry too much about exactly where their spices come from. They know that the so-called Spice Islands lie far beyond India, but that is all. By the end of the fifteenth century, however, spices have become as precious as gold! People are captivated by their intense aroma and flavour, as well as their exotic properties.

So, Europeans set sail, hoping to gain direct access to the Spice Islands for themselves.

This marks the beginning of the era of European exploration and colonisation: an era that will forever change our world.

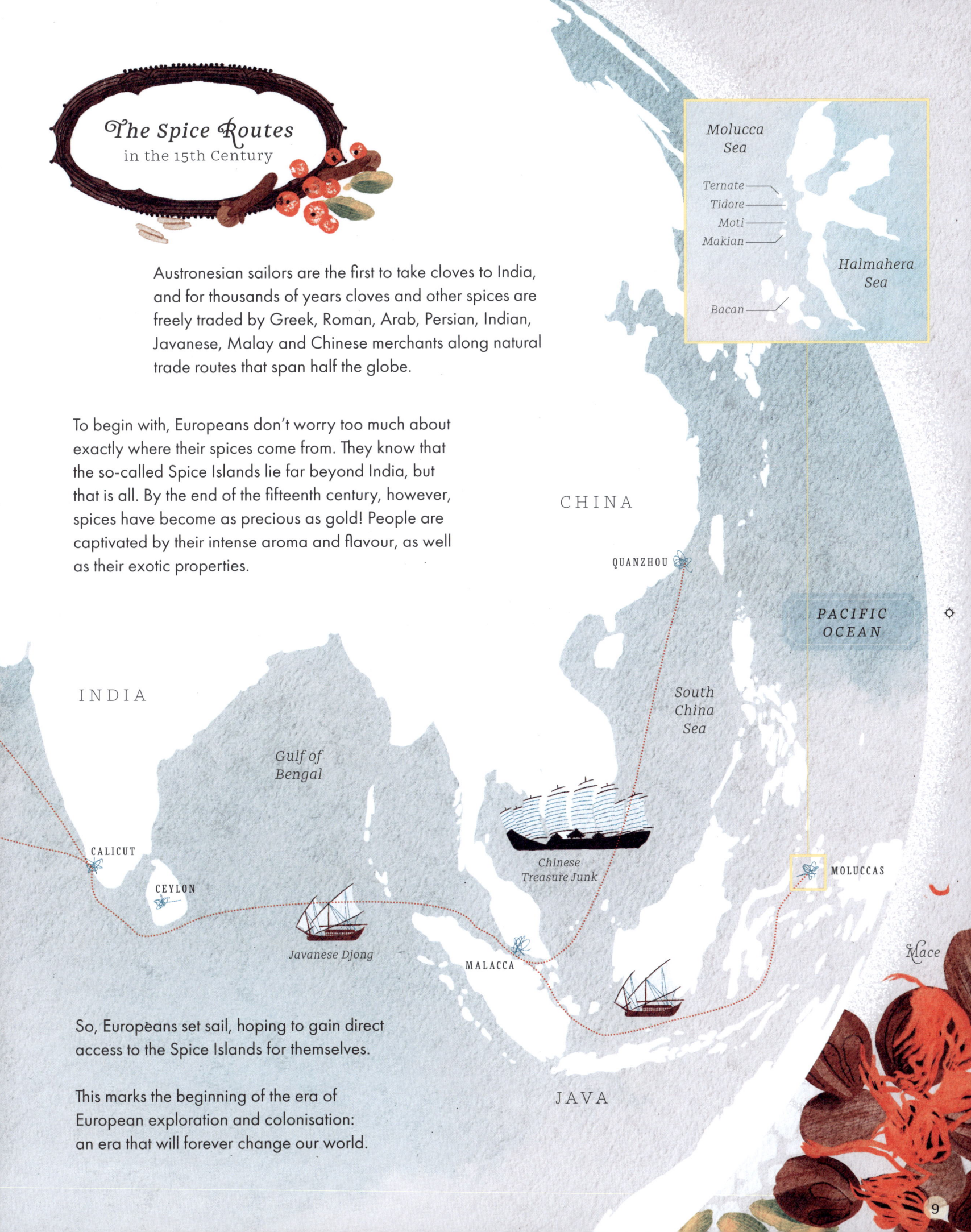

THE MARITIME RACE FOR SPICE

By the fifteenth century, the race to find a route from Europe to the Spice Islands is on! Portugal and Spain are vying for first place.

The Portuguese have improved their astronomical navigation techniques and developed new vessels which allow them to venture further into the ocean.

Caravel

Carrack

In 1488, Portuguese navigator Bartolomeu Dias successfully reaches the southern tip of Africa – now known as the Cape of Good Hope – establishing a crucial leg of the eastern sea route from Europe to India.

Meanwhile, Spain sends its ships westwards. In 1492, an expedition led by Italian explorer Christopher Columbus lands on what he thinks is the Indian mainland . . . but is, in fact, what is known today as the Americas – an entirely different continent!

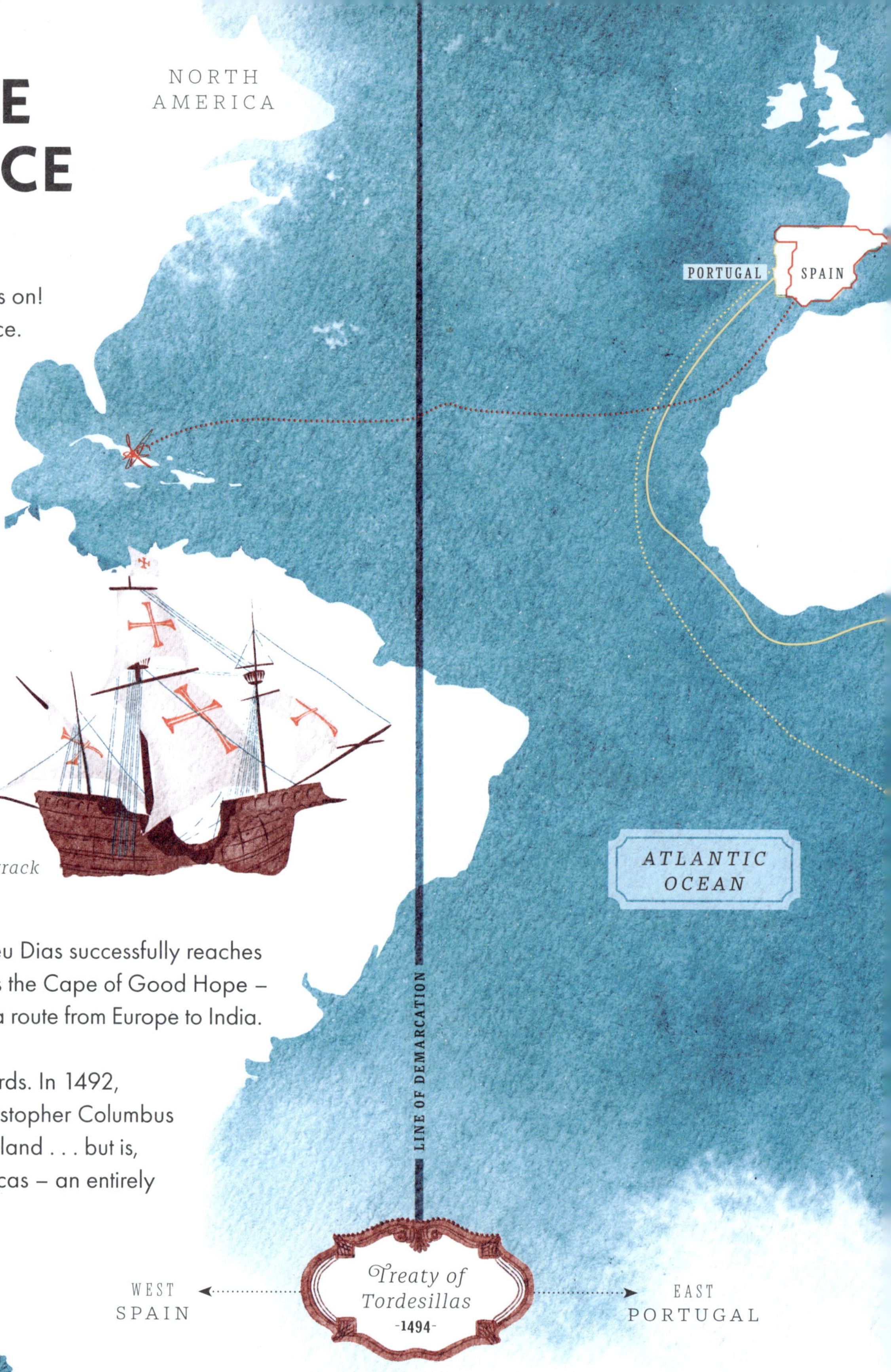

Bartolomeu Dias

Christopher Columbus

Vasco da Gama

NORTH AMERICA

PORTUGAL   SPAIN

ATLANTIC OCEAN

LINE OF DEMARCATION

Treaty of Tordesillas
-1494-

WEST
SPAIN

EAST
PORTUGAL

Tensions over land grow between Portugal and Spain and eventually they sign the Treaty of Tordesillas. With the support of the Pope, the two countries draw an imaginary line from the North Pole to the South Pole, dividing the world in two. All territories west of the line 'belong' to Spain, the treaty says, and those to the east 'belong' to Portugal.

The Portuguese continue their eastward advance on the Spice Islands, and Vasco da Gama reaches India in 1498. Then, in 1511, a Portuguese governor invades and takes control of the city of Malacca, an important point on the Spice Routes. The sea route to the Moluccas opens up.

Malacca (present-day Malaysia)

The Doctrine of Discovery

During the period often referred to as the Age of Exploration, many nations – not just Portugal and Spain – claimed ownership of lands that already belonged to others under the Doctrine of Discovery.

In 1493, the Pope issued a decree that said European Christian explorers could claim lands that already belonged to others. According to this decree, these explorers simply had to plant a flag in the soil, report the 'discovery' to their European ruler and occupy the land, and the land became theirs – whether someone was already there or not!

There were already people living in all of the places these European explorers went to. They all had their own nations, languages, cultures, religions and territories. When Europeans arrived and claimed a land, they were actually taking it from someone else. This had terrible consequences for Indigenous peoples in particular, whose land was stolen, and the world still feels the effects of it today.

Portugal has won the European race to the Spice Islands. But one question lingers in European minds: According to the treaty, who exactly do the Spice Islands 'belong' to – the Portuguese or the Spanish?

It still isn't clear where the dividing line runs on the opposite side of the planet . . . and for Europeans, that means the treasure of the spices is still to be claimed.

THE NAVIGATOR'S GAMBIT

The young King of Spain, Carlos I, can't see how his ships will ever reach the Spice Islands.

Carlos I (known as Charles V, Holy Roman Emperor)

How can they, when they are only allowed to set sail to the west? He deems the Moluccas unreachable.

Then, a Portuguese navigator suddenly appears before him.

"I have reached India twice with a Portuguese expedition via the eastern sea route," claims this navigator. "I possess not only experience in those foreign waters, but also knowledge of the exact location of the coveted islands. I can find a passage for Spain through the new continent."

This navigator is a defector, having turned his back on Portugal to offer his services to Spain . . . but he is promising the King another chance at the treasure. Might it really be possible to reach the Moluccas via a western sea route after all? And could it then be proven that the islands in fact fall under Spanish sovereignty?

The King cannot refuse this opportunity. His desire for the treasure of the spices is too great. He grants his approval for the navigator to lead a Spanish expedition.

INTO THE UNKNOWN

EUROPE
SPAIN

DATE 10 AUGUST 1519
DAYS 1
SAILORS VESSELS
240 5
37°23'19"N · 5°59'43"W
Seville

One year later, in September 1519, five ships set forth from the port of Seville. Laden with trinkets to trade, and provisions including enough ship's biscuits and wine for two years, the fleet embarks on a journey into uncharted waters, the sailors united under the banner of a singular idea: to reach the Spice Islands via a western sea route.

The provisions

10,000	kilograms of sea biscuit
200	tins of sardines
250	barrels of sherry
7	cows (to provide milk and fresh meat)
Plus . . .	garlic, herrings, figs, beans, lentils, rice, flour, cheese, honey, vinegar

As well as food, a collection of other items was also loaded on board, including candles, musical instruments, spare ship parts, tools, various objects to barter with (such as mirrors, scissors, knives, handkerchiefs, caps, bells, brass rings, pearls and fake gems) and weaponry (such as cannons, spears, crossbows, gunpowder, shields, shotguns and armour).

THE SAILORS

Aboard are approximately 240 men. They come from ten different nations, and they have no idea how long they will be gone, where they are going to go – or if they will ever return.

Their reasons for being on this expedition are varied. Some come in pursuit of a better life, drawn by the allure of great wealth or the opportunity to settle debts. Others have no choice, enslaved and forced to be there or compelled by circumstance. A tiny few are drawn by curiosity and the thirst for adventure.

ONE MISSION, MANY LANGUAGES

PORTUGAL
Fernão de Magalhães (Ferdinand Magellan) – The man with the plan

Born in Porto in 1480, de Magalhães began his career as an officer and navigator at age 25. He spent seven years travelling and fighting, reaching India twice and taking part in the 1511 capture of Malacca. When he returned to Lisbon in 1513, he fell out of favour with King Manuel I of Portugal and was dismissed from office. Feeling wronged, Magalhães turned his back on his country. In neighbouring Spain, he found a sympathetic ear in King Carlos I – and that is how a Portuguese navigator has found himself Captain-General of this Spanish fleet of five ships. He has spent the last few years planning this expedition down to the last detail.

ITALY
Antonio Pigafetta – The adventurous scribe

It is wanderlust that has prompted this young Venetian nobleman and student of astronomy and geography to join the expedition. Accepting the humble title of Supernumerary on a modest salary, he has boarded with his diary firmly in hand, ready to record everything that happens.

GREECE
Francisco Albo – The navigator's chronicle-keeper

Greek seaman Francisco Albo serves as the expedition's logbook-keeper. His responsibilities include documenting nautical information each day, and calculating and recording the fleet's position.

SOUTHEAST ASIA
Enrique of Malacca – The interpreter with hidden talents

Enrique is the name this man was given when he was baptised. Nobody knows his birth name, or even exactly where he was born. Enslaved and bought by Magellan in 1511, Enrique is aboard because he has no other choice. However, he has been officially enlisted as an interpreter, with a monthly salary of 1,500 maravedis. And, in his will, Magellan has expressed the desire that in the event of his death, Enrique be freed from slavery. The incredible value that Enrique will bring to this journey is yet to be revealed . . .

SPAIN
Juan Sebastián Elcano and Hernándo de Bustamante – The loyal companions

Born on the Spanish Basque coast, Juan Sebastián Elcano has the sea in his blood. Serving as a boatswain, Elcano embarks on this journey to seek pardon from King Carlos I, hoping to settle his legal debt. His companion Hernándo de Bustamante, a barber from Seville, serves as the ship's doctor.

SPAIN
Gonzalo Gómez de Espinosa – The hand of the law

The 44-year-old has been tasked with recruiting crew members for the mission. As Master-at-Arms, he is responsible for maintaining law and order, quelling riots and reading out punishments for those who break the ship's code.

SEA OF RIVALRY

On the 20th September, four stately carracks and a nimble caravel leave Sanlúcar de Barrameda and head out into the open sea. Already, things on board are unsettled.

The fact that Magellan, a Portuguese sailor, is leading a Spanish fleet does not sit well with the three Spanish captains.

Fore-topsail

Fore sail

Bowsprit

Spritsail

SAN ANTONIO

CREW: 57

23.83 m

CAPTAIN:	JUAN DE CARTAGENA
FREIGHT	COST
120 BARRELS	330.000 MARAVEDIS

CONCEPCIÓN

CREW: 44

22.05 m

CAPTAIN:	GASPAR DE QUESADA
FREIGHT	COST
90 BARRELS	228.750 MARAVEDIS

VICTORIA

CREW: 45

21.68 m

CAPTAIN:	LUIS DE MENDOZA
FREIGHT	COST
85 BARRELS	300.000 MARAVEDIS

It even seems King Carlos I himself may harbour some distrust, as he has appointed Juan de Cartagena overseer of the mission.

João Rodrigues Serrão, the Portuguese captain of the smallest ship, appears to be Magellan's only ally among the commanders.

Sensing the suspicious and scrutinising glares of the Spanish captains, Magellan acts boldly and with careful consideration from the outset.

GUIDING LIGHTS

So as not to lose the sense of direction in the vastness of the ocean, Magellan has the fleet sail in single file. At night, each ship lights a lantern at its stern to communicate with the others.

Navigation Tools

During early European voyages in the Atlantic, it became clear to sailors that they had to leave the coast to find the winds their ships needed to sail. To figure out where they were and travel safely in the correct direction, they needed new tools.

Initially, they used something called a quadrant to measure the height of the North Star in the sky. Later, they used the astrolabe and the cross-staff to work out the height of the Sun. These tools helped sailors to work out where they were, and made sailing safer. And, as the sailors developed their tools and improved their measurements, they also started to create more detailed maps of the world.

At night, sailors used the stars to navigate. But in the Southern Hemisphere, the stars are seen at a different angle. Constellations appear that cannot be seen in the north. To keep on course, sailors use the constellation they called the Southern Cross, whose long bar points the way to the South Pole.

Astrolabe

Magellan takes the lead in his flagship, the TRINIDAD. It is a clear signal to the other captains of who is in command.

The Captain-General is well aware that mistakes are not allowed. He knows this voyage will only succeed with absolute control and iron-clad discipline.

BECALMED AND BETRAYED

At this time, it is customary for European seafarers to cross the Atlantic with the trade winds, which blow from east to west – but Magellan commands his fleet to sail further south instead.

In doing so, he makes a bad decision, as even the most experienced sailors can. The ships enter calm waters near the equator, where the sailors find themselves stranded for weeks under scorching heat.

Outrage boils among the Spanish captains. The royal overseer, Cartagena, takes the opportunity to challenge Magellan's authority and provokes him several times – but the Captain-General makes it clear that disobedience will not be tolerated.

ARRIVAL IN THE JUNGLE BAY

SOUTH AMERICA
· BRAZIL ·

DATE — 13 DECEMBER 1519
DAYS — 126
SAILORS — VESSELS
239 — 5

22°47'25"S · 43°9'20"W

Rio de Janeiro

FORBIDDEN PARADISE

These Europeans are not the first that the Tupinambá have laid eyes on. Technically, the Spanish fleet is forbidden to anchor here, as the Portuguese have already been to this bay and 'claimed possession' of the land. But it is 1519, and no Portuguese settlements have been established yet, so the crew go ashore unhindered.

Cassava ('batatas')

The Tupinambá

Tupinambá was a name applied to a group of people that European sailors met in the late 1400s and early 1500s. They spoke Tupian languages and inhabited the eastern coast of modern-day Brazil.

Records from that time describe them having a rich culture of music, dance and ceramics, and a deep connection with nature. They believed that all elements of nature were inhabited by spirits, and their religious practices included rituals to give thanks for the harvest, ask for spiritual protection and honour ancestors.

Their tribes typically had about 200 people, sometimes up to 600. Villages had six to eight malocas, which were wicker huts with thatched roofs where they slept in hammocks. The Tupinambá hunted, gathered, fished and farmed, with cassava and corn as staple foods. Initially nomadic, they lived along the Brazilian coast. Their hand-carved canoes, made from a single piece of wood, allowed them to travel on rivers and the sea.

Lion Tamarin

Maloca

In 1500, Portugal took control of Brazil and pushed into the Amazon. Portuguese colonists enslaved and persecuted the Tupinambá, forcing them to move to remote areas to preserve their culture.

Brazil became independent in 1822, and Portuguese is still spoken there. Today, some Tupinambá remain in two regions and were officially recognized as Indigenous in 2002. Between 2004 and 2016, the Tupinambá of Olivença reclaimed about 90 farms as Indigenous lands.

Canoe

In his diary, Pigafetta documents his enchantment with this place. To him, it is a paradise. He vividly describes the local people, the parrots and lion tamarins he sees, and the delicacies he savours – tapir meat, 'batatas' and a 'sweet-tasting pine cone'.

Pineapple ('sweet-tasting pine cone')

Ceramics

Tapir

CURIOUS EXCHANGES

The Tupinambá barter enthusiastically with the European sailors.

A fishing hook in exchange for five or six chickens.
A mirror or scissors for enough fish to satisfy ten men.
A small bell for an entire basket of sweet potatoes.

Through this trade, the five ships are able to swiftly reload with firewood, fresh water and provisions.

A Hidden Trade

Sadly, it was more than hooks and trinkets that the visiting Europeans gave in their trade with the Indigenous peoples of countries such as Brazil. Unwittingly, they also brought diseases from their homelands – diseases that the Indigenous communities had never encountered, and therefore had little to no natural immunity to. This was devastating, resulting in the deaths of millions of Indigenous peoples.

Pigafetta is not the only one excited by this place. The other sailors, too, would love to stay longer . . .
but Magellan urges them onwards. After only two days, they resume their journey south along the coastline.

FROSTBITTEN HOPES

Magellan is convinced that there must be a passage from the east coast of South America through to the west, and that it must be near. He steers the fleet still further south, leaving behind the warm coast and lush forests of Brazil.

Cove by cove and day by day, the sailors try to find this longed-for passage.

Often, the nimble SANTIAGO is sent ahead, but the fleet repeatedly hits dead-ends in the form of land or narrow freshwater rivers.

On the 10th January 1520, the sailors come across a massive indentation in the coastline. This must be it! Full of hope, they sail into it, but eventually taste freshwater. They realise the mighty waterway is in fact a deep river estuary: The Río de la Plata. Disheartened, the sailors turn back.

It is a harsh blow for Magellan. He realises that the information on which he has based all his plans is incorrect. He tries not to show it, but for the first time he finds himself lacking conviction.

What if the western sea route to the Spice Islands doesn't exist after all?

There is only one thing left to do: continue south and hope to find success there.

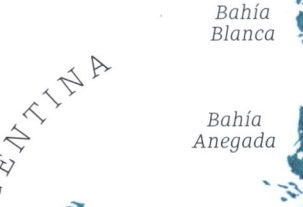

Bahía Blanca

Bahía Anegada

ARGENTINA

Golfo Nuevo

But the further south the ships sail, the more barren the coastline becomes. Apart from penguins on the shore and sea lions basking on the cliffs, the sailors see no other sign of life.

Months pass and winter sets in, with the days growing ever shorter and icy storms assailing the fleet. Cruel winds batter the hulls and masts of the ships. The sailors' hands, feet and noses are permanently frozen. What little hope and enthusiasm remains among the sailors wanes, while cold and hunger gnaw at their strength.

San Julián

Magellan cloaks himself in silence. His intentions become increasingly unclear. On and on they sail, and still there is no sign of the coveted passage through the continent . . .

33

MUTINY AND MISFORTUNE

Magellan's hand is forced. The condition of both his fleet and his men brings the expedition to a halt, and in March 1520 he decides to winter in the bay of San Julián.

Half a year has passed since the fleet set off from Spain . . . but not one of the promises made to the sailors has materialised.

SOUTH AMERICA
ARGENTINA

DATE	31 MARCH 1520
DAYS	235
SAILORS	VESSELS
237	5
49°18'0"S · 67°43'0"W	

Puerto San Julián

So, when Magellan reduces the food rations, the discontent among the men reaches a fever pitch. The Spanish captains seize the opportunity to bring the journey to an end.

They press Magellan to reveal his plans, but he refuses to admit defeat. He will not stop believing . . . He has come too far to give up now.

On the 2nd April, a mutiny erupts during the night. Led by the liberated Cartagena, the Spanish captains take control of the SAN ANTONIO and hand command over to Elcano. All they have to do to persuade the other hungry men to join them is open the pantry.

Soon, three out of the five ships are defying Magellan's commands.

But by the next morning, in a clever counterstrike achieved with the help of a few loyal men – including Gonzalo Gómez de Espinosa – Magellan has regained control of all five ships!

Shortly after the mutiny, Magellan sends the SANTIAGO on an exploration mission to the south. But the ship gets caught in a storm and drifts, badly damaged, toward the coast. One enslaved man drowns.

Captain Serrão manages to steer the ship onto a sandbank, allowing the crew to reach land before the ship crashes into a cliff and is lost.

They are about 150 kilometres away from San Julián. The 33 shipwreck survivors begin the arduous journey back on foot along the coast, battling freezing nights and strong winds. They survive on mussels and roots, drinking dew from leaves.

Nearly a whole month passes, but in the end, the entire crew is rescued.

AN INHUMANE DECEIT

One day, an extremely tall man appears in the bay. Pigafetta writes in his diary that this man is throwing dust in his hair, dancing and singing.

Magellan sends some of his men ashore to mimic the man's gestures in order to gain his trust. They also give him a comb, glass beads and a mirror. When the man sees his own reflection, he falls in shock, knocking over four men in the process.

This is the first time Europeans have made contact with the Indigenous Tehuelche people of Patagonia. The Europeans go on to make many more attempts at communication, but most Tehuelche avoid contact with them.

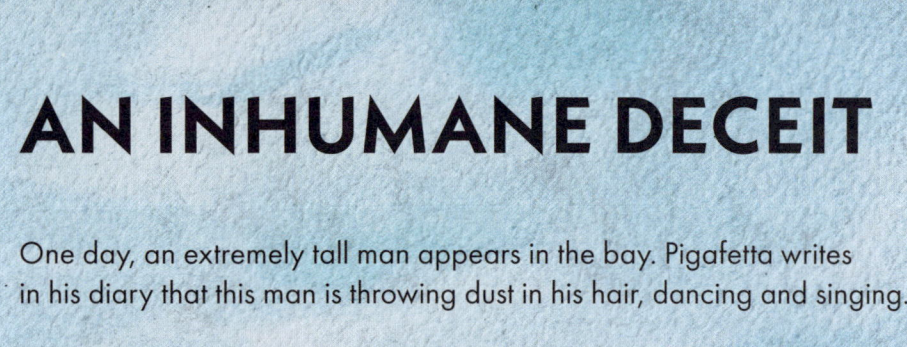

The Tehuelche

Originally, the Tehuelche were hunter-gatherers. The men always carried bows and arrows and were excellent marksmen. Everything else was carried by the women on their backs. They were excellent hunters of guanaco (a mammal related to the llama that is native to South America), which were still abundant at that time. The Tehuelche ate the raw meat, then used the hides for their clothing and shelters. They lived in large, relatively open tents made of strong branches and covered with guanaco hides. They also covered their bodies with sewn-together animal skins, wearing them with the soft side inward and tying them at the waist with a band.

At around 1.9 metres, the Tehuelche were considerably taller than the European sailors, who would have been 30–40 centimetres shorter on average. Magellan gave the people of this coast the name Patagonians, and for centuries reports of them fuelled the imagination of Europeans, who truly believed that giants lived here, as Pigafetta had described.

One day, Magellan decides he wants to bring two strong, young Tehuelche men aboard so he can take them to Spain as proof of their existence. But, of course, these men do not want to go.

So, Magellan deceives them. He has so many mirrors, knives and glass beads brought to them that their hands are full. Then, two sets of foot shackles are also presented as 'gifts'.

When the Tehuelche men realise that they have been tricked, they are furious. They scream and cry, but Magellan shows no mercy. He keeps them captive. One is brought aboard the SAN ANTONIO, the other aboard the VICTORIA. The two men will never see their homeland again.

Explorers or kidnappers?

When European explorers encountered people they'd never seen before, it was common for them to try to kidnap them as Magellan did the Tehuelche men. This is because they saw the people they were encountering as items of interest rather than fellow human beings. These kidnapped people were ripped away from their own homes and cultures, taken halfway across the world, and then cruelly presented to monarchs alongside objects such as gold and spices as examples of the great 'riches' to be obtained in future expeditions.

STORMS AND SALTWATER

With winter relinquishing its hold, the remaining four ships finally depart the ill-fated San Julián Bay on the 24th August 1520, and their journey into the unknown continues. As for the instigators of the mutiny? Some were killed outright, while others were left behind in the bay, never to be seen again.

After only a few weeks, the ships are forced to seek refuge from furious storms, and remain stranded for another two months.

Little do the sailors know, they are in a spot closer to the passage than they could ever imagine . . .

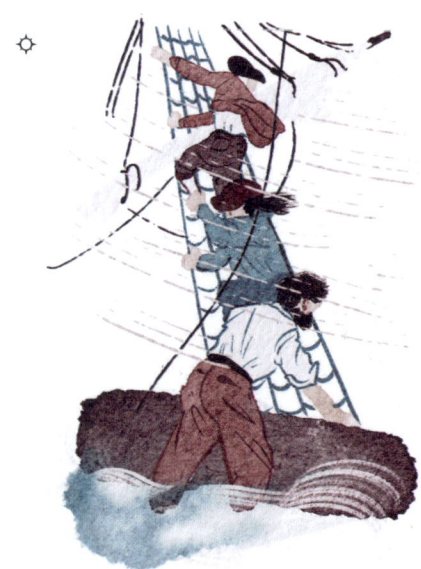

On the 21st October, they set sail once more, and just three days later, they see it: a headland with white cliffs rising from the otherwise flat, desolate coast, and behind it a deep bay. But as the VICTORIA and the CONCEPCIÓN venture further ahead, a storm looms. The two ships are driven deeper into the bay and disappear.

ATLANTIC OCEAN

San Julián

Puerto Santa Cruz

Cabo Vírgenes

ARGENTINA

For days, the TRINIDAD and the SAN ANTONIO anxiously await a signal. Then, just when they think the ships must have shattered against the rocks, they spy smoke rising in the distance.

The waiting ships rush forward, expecting to find shipwrecked sailors, but instead they see the VICTORIA and the CONCEPCIÓN with their sails raised, triumphantly firing their cannons. "Saltwater!" the joyous cries ring out over the water.

Guanaco

This is it! The waterway they have been searching for! The exit is yet to be revealed, but this is certainly not a river . . .
Supplies are running low, and the ships need repairs, but Magellan presses the fleet onward.

LOST IN THE MAZE

CHILE

Like a labyrinth, the way forward unfolds before them, but no one knows which of the many channels will lead them to the exit.

Magellan relies on his keen senses as a seafarer. He dispatches his men in dinghies to explore the area, and whenever the sailors report that a branch continues, the larger ships close in and search for a safe anchorage. Time and again, the fleet divides, navigating the maze of branches, twists and dead-ends to find the right exit, and skilfully manoeuvring through the shallows of sandbanks, islands and peninsulas.

CABO DESEADO

Kawésqar

PACIFIC OCEAN

SARDINE BAY

Slowly, the fleet makes its way through the rugged landscape. It is a world of stone and ice. There is hardly anything growing on the coast, but in the distance rise dense forests and white-capped mountains. There seems to be no trace of human life, but at night the flames of campfires dance along the shore.

Magellan Penguin

The Strait of Magellan

The passage connecting the Atlantic and Pacific Oceans still bears Magellan's name today. Due to its narrowness, and the unpredictable tidal currents and winds, it is considered one of the most difficult routes to navigate in the world. As a result, this sea route never brought the benefits that the Spanish had hoped for; the route was too dangerous and too far from Europe for rapid transport of goods. Nevertheless, it remained an important shipping route until the Panama Canal was opened in 1914. Today, the nearly 600-kilometre-long Strait of Magellan, with its many islands and branches in southern Chile, is a natural paradise.

ATLANTIC OCEAN

CABO VÍRGENES

From the boats, it is impossible to find the way, so the men go ashore and climb the hills to try to find the exit. The fleet anchors in a sheltered place – so-called 'Sardine Bay' – and the men catch fresh fish, gather mussels and forage the celery that sprouts beside drinkable water.

ARGENTINA

Selk'nam

Tierra del Fuego

Tierra del Fuego – the Land of Fire – is the name Magellan gave to the island group located in the south and separated from the mainland by the sea route. This name refers to the many burning campfires sighted by sailors at night. The Indigenous hunters and gatherers living there had settled and inhabited the southern tip of South America for thousands of years. Four Indigenous groups settled on Tierra del Fuego: the Yámana, the Haush, the Selk'nam and the Kawésqar. Today, there are no surviving Haush peoples, and very few Yámana. However, the Kawésqar are a nationally recognised Indigenous group in Chile, and descendants of the Selk'nam live in Agentina and Chile.

Tierra del Fuego

Yámana

Haush

Then, one day, the SAN ANTONIO disappears. For days, the sailors look for the lost ship, leaving messages and even sending a search party back to the entrance of the strait. But it is all in vain.

The SAN ANTONIO – the largest ship with the most provisions on board – has secretly deserted them. It has already set its course back to Spain. There are 57 sailors on board, and one of the kidnapped Tehuelche men, who will tragically die from heat as the ship crosses the Atlantic.

TEARS OF TRIUMPH

On the 13th November 1520, two young sailors – one of whom is Hernándo de Bustamante – climb the rocks and together catch sight of the opening from the strait.

The way out is found!

Amid the joyful thundering of the artillery, the usually closed-off and relentless Magellan is overcome by emotion. Unable to hold it back, he weeps before the entire crew. Tears of joy and relief.

Everything he so deeply believed in has now come true.

THE WIDE BLUE YONDER

The three remaining ships exit the strait and sail into a vast blue expanse. Guided by steady trade winds, the fleet sets a course northwest, leaving the cool southern regions for warmer realms.

South America
- CHILE -

DATE	28 NOVEMBER 1520
DAYS	477
SAILORS	VESSELS
166	3

52°43'51"S · 74°43'39"W

Cabo Deseado

The storms subside, and before the sailors stretches a seemingly endless and tranquil ocean, unexplored from the east by any European before.

Magellan dubs it Mar Pacífico – the calm and peaceful sea.

ADRIFT IN THE KNOWN UNKNOWN

Too calm! After almost a hundred days, the sailors still have not seen a single island.

In fact, there are countless islands in this ocean, but Magellan and his fleet unknowingly sail past all of them. The Pacific Ocean is not as tranquil as it seems. On the contrary, it can be quite stormy, and its waterways have bustled with maritime traffic for millennia.

Polynesian Seafarers

Since long before Magellan named it the Pacific, this great blue expanse has been known by other names. For example, Hawaiians call it Moananuiākea, and in Māori it is Te Moana-nui-a-Kiwa.

Polynesian seafarers set sail on this vast ocean 3,000 years ago, and ventured out into it time and again. They travelled great distances with no need for tools such as compasses. Instead, they used precise knowledge of the stars to find their way. Also guided by the wind direction, currents and the flight of birds, these excellent navigators sailed Moananuiākea in ocean-going outrigger canoes and landed on hundreds of islands in the process. From New Guinea and the Philippines, they voyaged to – and settled on – the extensive array of islands between New Zealand and Hawai'i. As a result, all the inhabitable islands had long been settled by the time the Europeans arrived in the region.

But, lacking charts and the necessary knowledge, Magellan and his crew find themselves adrift in unfamiliar waters. Days turn into weeks, then months, and all the while the ships sail under relentless heat with the same unchanging view.

DESOLATE SEAS

Food supplies dwindle. The drinking water begins to taste brackish and give off a foul odour. The ship's biscuits, riddled with maggots, turn to powder. The starving sailors chew on old leather straps from the rigging, hardened by sun and salt. If luck is on their side, they come across an equally famished rat to kill and eat . . .

Malnourished and suffering from hunger and thirst, first one sailor then another falls ill. Day by day, their numbers dwindle. For many, including the second kidnapped Tehuelche man, the sea becomes their grave.

Scurvy

Between the fifteenth and eighteenth centuries, around two million sailors died of scurvy. It is caused by a lack of vitamin C, and was common at this time due to the unbalanced diet of sailors spending months at sea. General weakness, loss of muscle and bone pain are followed by bleeding gums and tooth loss, which is why its name means 'mouth rot'. It was not until the eighteenth century that it was discovered that citrus fruits could prevent the disease.

SHADOWS ON THE SHORE

After more than 13,000 nautical miles and 105 days adrift on the Pacific, the fleet finally reaches land – the islands known today as the Marianas.

The local CHamoru people swiftly approach the exhausted sailors on their agile sakman. Pigafetta later writes in his diary, "Their outrigger boats passed our ship very quickly, even though we were under full sail . . . They are like dolphins jumping from wave to wave."

OCEANIA
· MARIANAS ·
DATE — 6 MARCH 1521
DAYS — 575
SAILORS — 147
VESSELS — 3
13°27'40"N · 144°40'12"E
Guam

The CHamoru initiate trade: goods in exchange for fresh provisions.

The CHamoru

Like Pigafetta, the Europeans who came to the Mariana Islands in the sixteenth and seventeenth centuries were impressed by the hundreds of sailing canoes that met their ships at sea, surrounded them and sailed around them at speeds two to three times faster than their fastest ships. This is how the CHamoru's sakman became known in Europe as 'flying proas'.

However, when Spanish soldiers and missionaries established a permanent settlement on Guam in 1668, they forced all CHamoru from the northern islands to move there, where many died of European diseases. The Spanish also killed many CHamoru, and burned their sakman to try to make them lose their seafaring traditions. They wanted to destroy CHamoru culture, and to stop the CHamoru from ever leaving the island.

The CHamoru invented and sailed the fastest sailing ships in the world, but by around 1800 very few remained who still knew this. Since then, though, the CHamoru have fought to restore their culture and numbers. Many continue to live in the Mariana Islands, and there are still more who live in several states of the United States of America.

However, trouble brews when a group of islanders takes one of the Europeans' dinghies. Magellan, who deems the dinghy indispensable, feels robbed. He forcefully retrieves it, then in retribution orders several settlements along the coast to be set on fire – even though these same islanders spared him and his sailors from certain death.

Then, in a final blow before departing, he dubs their home 'Islas de los Ladrones' – the Islands of Thieves.

WHISPERS OF THE ARCHIPELAGO

Several days later, the fleet reaches the present-day Philippines. Here, their pilot, Francisco Albo, checks his calculations and determines that they have crossed the Treaty of Tordesillas line. They have unwittingly sailed right into Portuguese territory . . . and that also means the coveted Moluccas fall in Portuguese territory, too!

Magellan's mission has failed. He realises he cannot fulfill his promise to the Spanish king, because the treasure of the spices has gone to Portugal. And, in the eyes of the Portuguese king, he is considered a traitor. How can he ever return home?

South East Asia
PHILIPPINES
DATE — 16 MARCH 1521
DAYS — 584
SAILORS — 146
VESSELS — 3
10°44'0"N · 125°43'0"E
Homonhon

His crew has now been travelling for eighteen months. The ships are in poor condition, and the surviving men heavily fatigued. They need to recover before they encounter the Portuguese, and Magellan needs time to think.

They establish a camp on a sheltered island, and the stronger among them to set out to find food. They return from the palm groves with coconuts, and the juice and flesh of these tropical fruits revives the weary and exhausted sailors.

Then, people adorned from head to toe with gold accessories and tattoos appear. These are the Visayan, one of the Indigenous groups of the area. When Magellan extends a handful of cloves with a questioning look, they tell him where he can find more treasures. Magellan's interest is piqued.

The Golden Age

When the first Spaniards arrived on the islands now called the Philippines, they saw many people wearing gold jewellery. Not much is known about these people, but one thing is for sure: they were amazingly skilled goldsmiths. Gold was always plentiful in the Philippines, and both men and women from all social classes wore it as necklaces, earrings, bracelets, armlets and belts. Sword and dagger handles were also made of gold.

These treasures were passed down through generations or buried with their owners to take to the afterlife. The Spanish colonists not only destroyed these people's culture, but also took their gold for themselves.

ECHOES OF CONQUEST AND RESISTANCE

The fleet voyages deeper into the Philippines archipelago, coming across many inhabited islands unknown to Europeans.

Here, Magellan sees an opportunity: he could form alliances with powerful rulers and negotiate trade agreements for Spain. Then he discovers that his enslaved interpreter, Enrique, is familiar with Malay, the local language of trade.

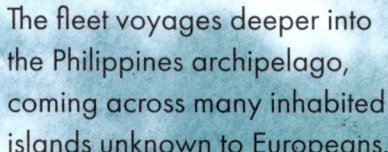

Enrique teaches Magellan the culture and the language, and acts as a mediator between the Captain-General and Rajah Colambu, the tribal leader of the island of Limasawa.

Impressed by the Spanish fleet's armour and cannons, Colambu guides them to a nearby island called Cebu, which is ruled by the even more powerful Rajah Humabon.

The fleet arrives in Cebu on the 7th April 1521. The island is part of an intricate trading network, and Rajah Humabon sees these Europeans as promising trading partners.

At first Humabon expects Magellan to pay a tax to trade here, but Enrique knows Magellan would never agree to this. He makes it clear: free trade or war! And so, Humabon agrees.

Instead, the two leaders make a blood pact. They will help each other during planting, harvesting and especially war. Magellan suggests that the Cebu ruler embrace the Christian faith to show submission to the King of Spain. In return, Rajah Humabon will be declared the most powerful king in the region. Other islands will pay tribute to him and benefit from the Spanish king's protection. Humabon agrees, and 800 island residents are baptised in a solemn ceremony.

However, not all the islanders welcome these Europeans meddling in their daily lives. On the small neighbouring island of Mactan, Datu Lapulapu resists and will not obey foreign orders. Magellan threatens to teach Lapulapu a lesson, and demonstrate Spain's strength . . .

But Lapulapu is undeterred. If Magellan wants to fight, then he should come and fight!

THE UNYIELDING SHORE

Lapulapu needs neither cannons nor iron armour. He understands the nature of his island and knows how to use it to his advantage.

Magellan has no such knowledge. When he sets out for the island of Mactan in the early morning, his large ships cannot approach the coast, because it is surrounded by a coral reef and the tide is too low.

The fleet is forced to anchor offshore, much too far away to fire the cannons. Instead, Magellan and 59 armed men row towards the island in three boats, then wade through the last stretch of knee-deep water to the beach in their cumbersome armour.

This is what Lapulapu is waiting for. He and his 1,500 fearless and resolute warriors are ready to defend their island from these foreigners.

They shoot arrows and bamboo spears, and hurl sharpened sticks and stones. It is a terrible massacre. The Europeans are clearly outnumbered, and Magellan orders his men to retreat.

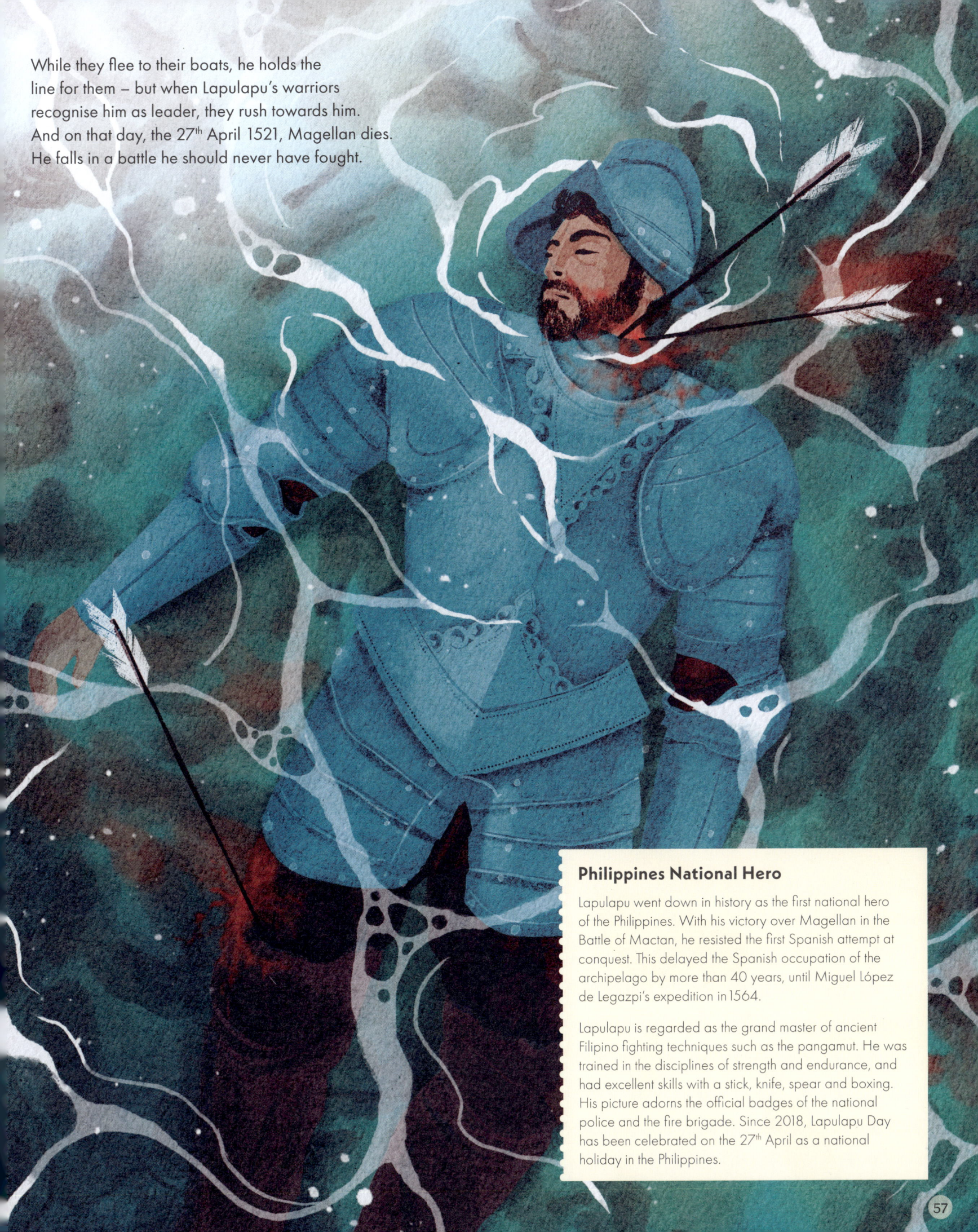

While they flee to their boats, he holds the line for them – but when Lapulapu's warriors recognise him as leader, they rush towards him. And on that day, the 27th April 1521, Magellan dies. He falls in a battle he should never have fought.

Philippines National Hero

Lapulapu went down in history as the first national hero of the Philippines. With his victory over Magellan in the Battle of Mactan, he resisted the first Spanish attempt at conquest. This delayed the Spanish occupation of the archipelago by more than 40 years, until Miguel López de Legazpi's expedition in 1564.

Lapulapu is regarded as the grand master of ancient Filipino fighting techniques such as the pangamut. He was trained in the disciplines of strength and endurance, and had excellent skills with a stick, knife, spear and boxing. His picture adorns the official badges of the national police and the fire brigade. Since 2018, Lapulapu Day has been celebrated on the 27th April as a national holiday in the Philippines.

THE BETRAYAL

When Rajah Humabon witnesses Magellan's catastrophic defeat, he sees that these foreigners, with their armour and their weapons, are not invincible. Doubt starts to creep in, and the ruler decides to invite the remaining sailors to one last grand feast.

As for Enrique, he is technically a free man. According to Magellan's will, he is to be released from his duties after ten years of enslavement. However, Enrique has become indispensable to the crew. He is the only one familiar with the languages and cultures of these lands. The fleet's new commanders refuse Enrique his freedom.

When the sailors receive the invitation to Rajah Humabon's feast, 26 accept. But it is no feast – it is an ambush by the King of Cebu!

Only a few sailors manage to escape to their ships. For most, including the fleet's new commanders, this is the end of the journey. Afterwards, Enrique is also missing . . . but has he been killed, or could he have escaped unnoticed in the chaos? Or was he, as Pigafetta suspects, involved in the betrayal?

The sailors never hear of Enrique again, but one thing remains certain to this day: he travelled far enough in one direction that he reached a point where his own language was spoken. He had apparently returned to the place he'd come from – or, to put it another way, he'd voyaged all the way round the world. And, in this way, he can be considered the first person known to achieve a complete circumnavigation of the globe!

A LEADERLESS CREW

In the ambush, the crew loses almost all of its officers and helmsmen. A heavy burden. Hurriedly, the 113 remaining men prepare to leave the island of Cebu.

They are too few to continue with three ships, so they set the CONCEPCIÓN – which is in particularly bad condition after two years at sea – ablaze. Melancholy seizes the sailors as they depart.

One of the helmsmen takes command, but things soon descend into chaos. It is clear that Magellan's successor lacks the necessary nautical knowledge, and it seems the fleet's moral compass has died with their Captain-General.

The once-royal fleet turns into a pirate gang, plundering passing boats, looting islands and capturing people. For a full seven months, the sailors meander onwards in this manner through the island maze.

But two sailors eventually step out of the shadows and put an end to the misconduct. Gonzalo Gómez de Espinosa takes command of the TRINIDAD, while Sebastián Elcano takes the VICTORIA.

This strong duo resumes the fleet's mission, and embarks once again on the search for the Spice Islands.

But without Enrique by their side, communication is challenging, and it is only with the forced help of captured fishermen and pilots that they can find the right path . . .

THE END OF THE QUEST

In the afternoon of the 8th November 1521, after 820 days at sea, the two remaining Spanish carracks drop anchor about 200 metres from the tiny volcanic island of Tidore.

They are right at the equator, at the other end of the world from their own home. Hot air shimmers over the forested mountain slopes, echoing the cannons' salute.

SOUTH EAST ASIA
Indonesia

DATE	8 NOVEMBER 1521
DAYS	820
SAILORS	VESSELS
90	2

0°40'43" · 127°26'53"E

Tidore

Finally, the sailors have found the treasure trove of spices. They have arrived. Here, in the Moluccas!

WHERE THE CLOVE TREE GROWS

SCALE: 1 : 100,000

0 1 2 3 4 5 Miles

TERNATE

TIDORE

A delicate fragrance hangs in the humid air. Not far from each other, two small volcanic cones – perfectly round and covered in lush green – rise from the sea. Surrounded by a jagged barrier reef, they stand at a distance, protected from the intrusion of unwelcome guests. These are the twin islands of Ternate and Tidore: The home of the clove tree.

Long ago, Chinese and Arab traders found their way to these islands. These nations understand the value of cloves, and through trading the spice, have become magnificent civilisations.

The Spanish fleet spends at least four to five days at anchor, then Sultan Al-Mansur of Tidore paddles over in a kora-kora.

The sultan has his own interpreter, and promptly engages in negotiations with the Spaniards.

Kora-kora

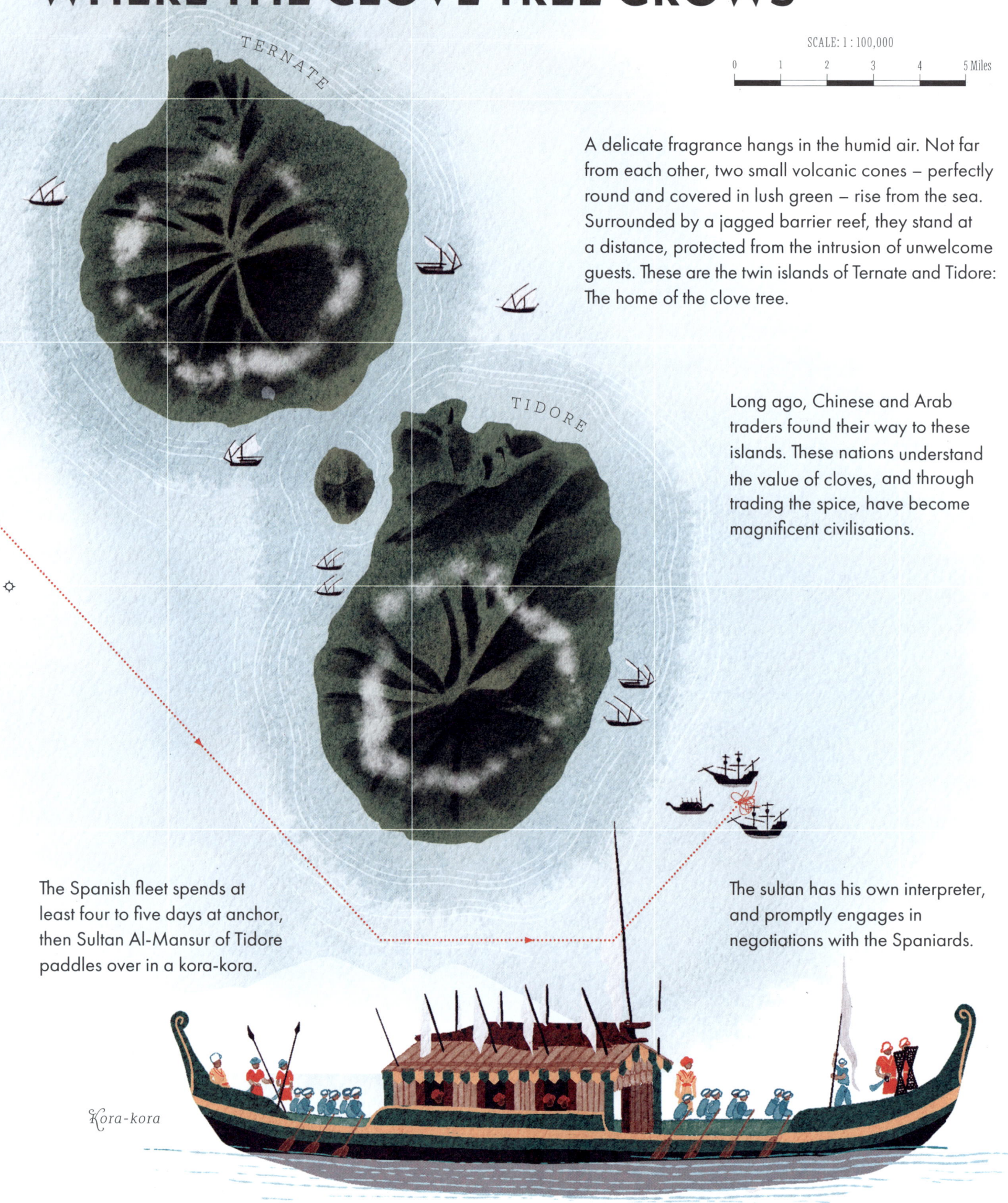

He is pleased with their arrival, and ready to sell them shiploads of his precious cloves! But, above all, the sultan desires a strong alliance with the strangers from the west.

Sultan Bayan Sirrullah of the neighbouring island of Ternate has grown even more powerful in recent years under the influence of the Portuguese, and Sultan Al-Mansur hopes for protection against this rival.

The pact is sealed.

Spanish goods are exchanged for sacks full of cloves until the ships are fully loaded. The Spanish fleet has achieved the goal of its long journey.

The Moluccas

The Moluccas were at the beginning of what is now Indonesia. Magellan's former companion and friend, Francisco Serrão, had reached the islands of Ternate in 1512, and formed an alliance with Sultan Bayan Sirrullah of Ternate. It was from Serrão that Magellan had learnt where these islands were.

Wanting to control the spice trade, Portugal built fortresses throughout the islands. In 1529, they made an agreement with Spain, called the Treaty of Saragossa, that let Spain control the Philippines. In exchange, Portugal kept control of the Spice Islands. Then, in the seventeenth century, the Dutch arrived and took over. They moved the centre of clove administration to the island of Ambon and had all the trees on Ternate felled. The island of Banda Neira, the birthplace of nutmeg, suffered an even crueller fate: everyone who lived on the island was killed in 1621.

However, in the eighteenth century, Ternate, Tidore and the Banda Islands were forgotten when Frenchman Pierre Poivre stole clove and nutmeg plants, and planted them on Mauritius and Zanzibar.

It was only in 1945 that almost 350 years of colonial rule by the Dutch came to an end, and Indonesia was declared independent.

However, the power struggle over cloves has just begun. Europeans will wage this battle at the other end of the world for centuries to come.

DIVERGENT PATHS

Planning their return to Europe, Espinosa and Elcano decide to split the risk by setting sail in two different directions. Espinosa will sail east, leading the TRINIDAD back across the Pacific. Meanwhile, Elcano will try to steer the VICTORIA home by heading westwards through Portuguese territory.

Before Espinosa can set sail again, the flagship needs repairs. Only in April 1522 does it finally depart eastward, with 48 men aboard, laden with spices and supplies. However, in the Pacific Ocean, the crew encounters extraordinarily strong storms. For weeks, they battle typhoons, scurvy and hunger, until all seems hopeless.

With only 20 exhausted men remaining, Espinosa turns back towards the Moluccas, but in the meantime a second Portuguese fleet has arrived in Ternate. Before Espinosa and his men can reach the coast, they are captured and enslaved by the Portuguese.

The TRINIDAD succumbs to its damages and sinks in the bay of Ternate. Only Espinosa and three other crew members end up surviving, and don't make their way back to Europe until years later.

Elcano embarks on his journey immediately, leaving on the 21st December 1521 with 47 men. Some of the sultan's local guides lead them through the Indonesian archipelago to the island of Timor, where they replenish their supplies one last time.

They have over 8,000 nautical miles still ahead of them before they reach home, but a stopover is impossible. To remain unnoticed by the Portuguese, they must sail far off the coast. After three months, they circumvent the Cape of Good Hope at the southern tip of the African continent, battling storms for eleven days and losing the VICTORIA's foremast.

The ship is badly in need of repair and struggles across the Atlantic Ocean, with hunger and scurvy only adding to the crew's challenges. Water seeps into the cargo holds, and the men pump day and night, trying desperately to keep the ship afloat . . .

THE SOLE STOP

AFRICA
- CAPE VERDE -

DATE — 9 JULY 1522
DAYS — 1,065
SAILORS — 34
VESSELS — 1
14°55'0"N · 23°36'15"W

Cidade Velha

After half a year at sea, the exhausted crew is forced to make a stopover at Cape Verde – but these islands fall within Portuguese territory as well.

Twelve members go ashore, pretending to be American, to try to trade for fresh provisions. But their lie is exposed, and the Portuguese capture the group.

Elcano and the remaining sailors hastily depart, vanishing from the island with the supplies.

TRIUMPH AND TRAGEDY

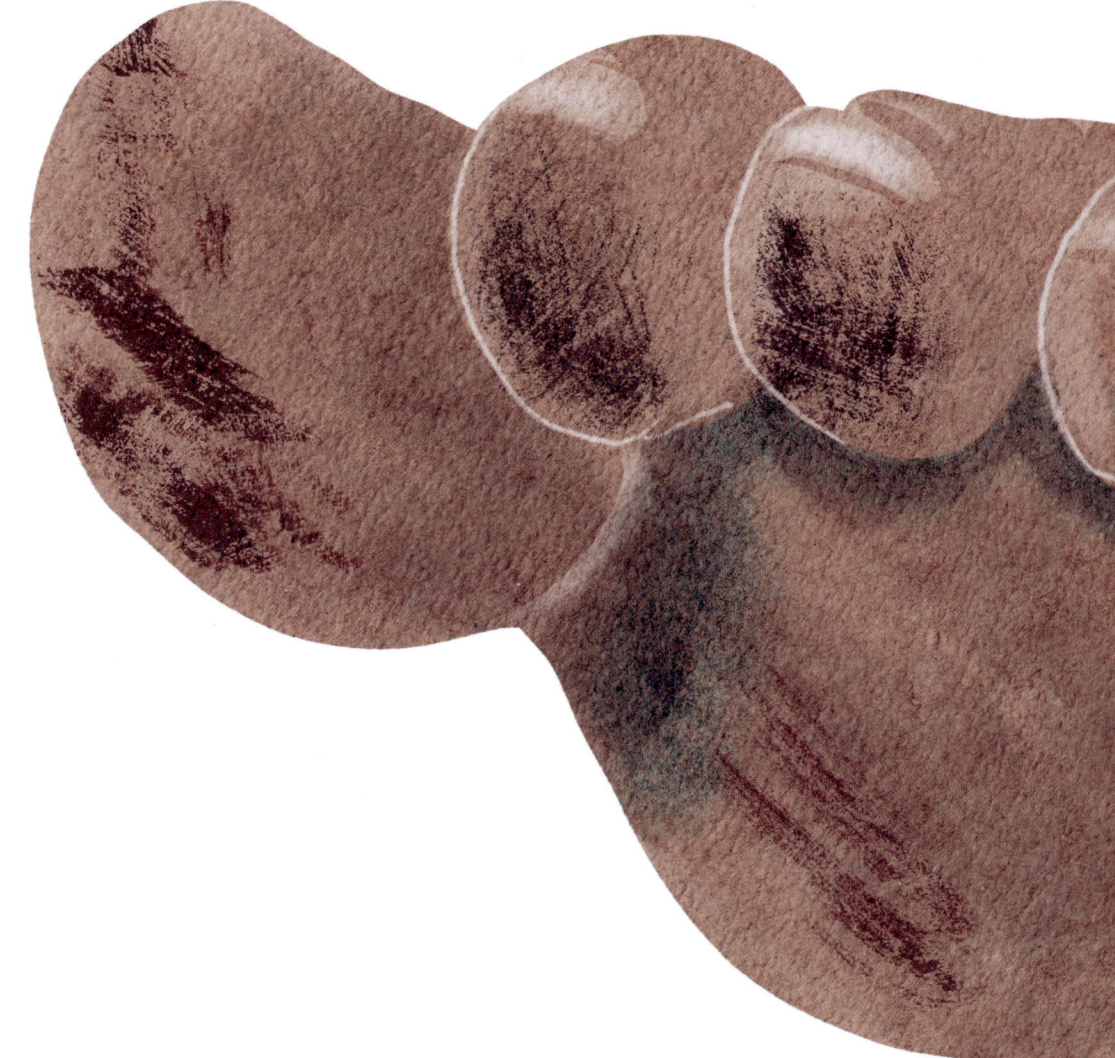

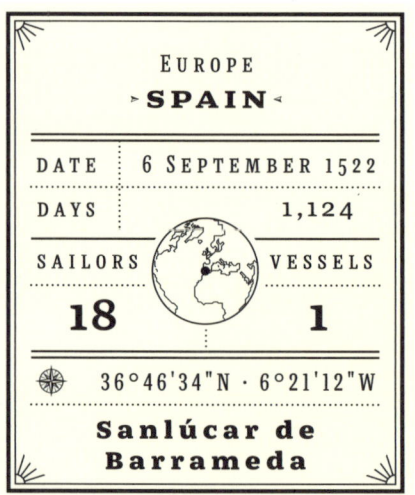

EUROPE
· SPAIN ·

DATE	6 SEPTEMBER 1522
DAYS	1,124
SAILORS	VESSELS
18	1

36°46'34"N · 6°21'12"W

Sanlúcar de Barrameda

On the 6th September 1522, a ship resembling a ghostly apparition docks in the Spanish port of Sanlúcar de Barrameda, near Seville.

The sailors aboard appear more dead than alive. Emaciated and sick, they use their last remaining strength to step upon the ground they left behind nearly three years earlier.

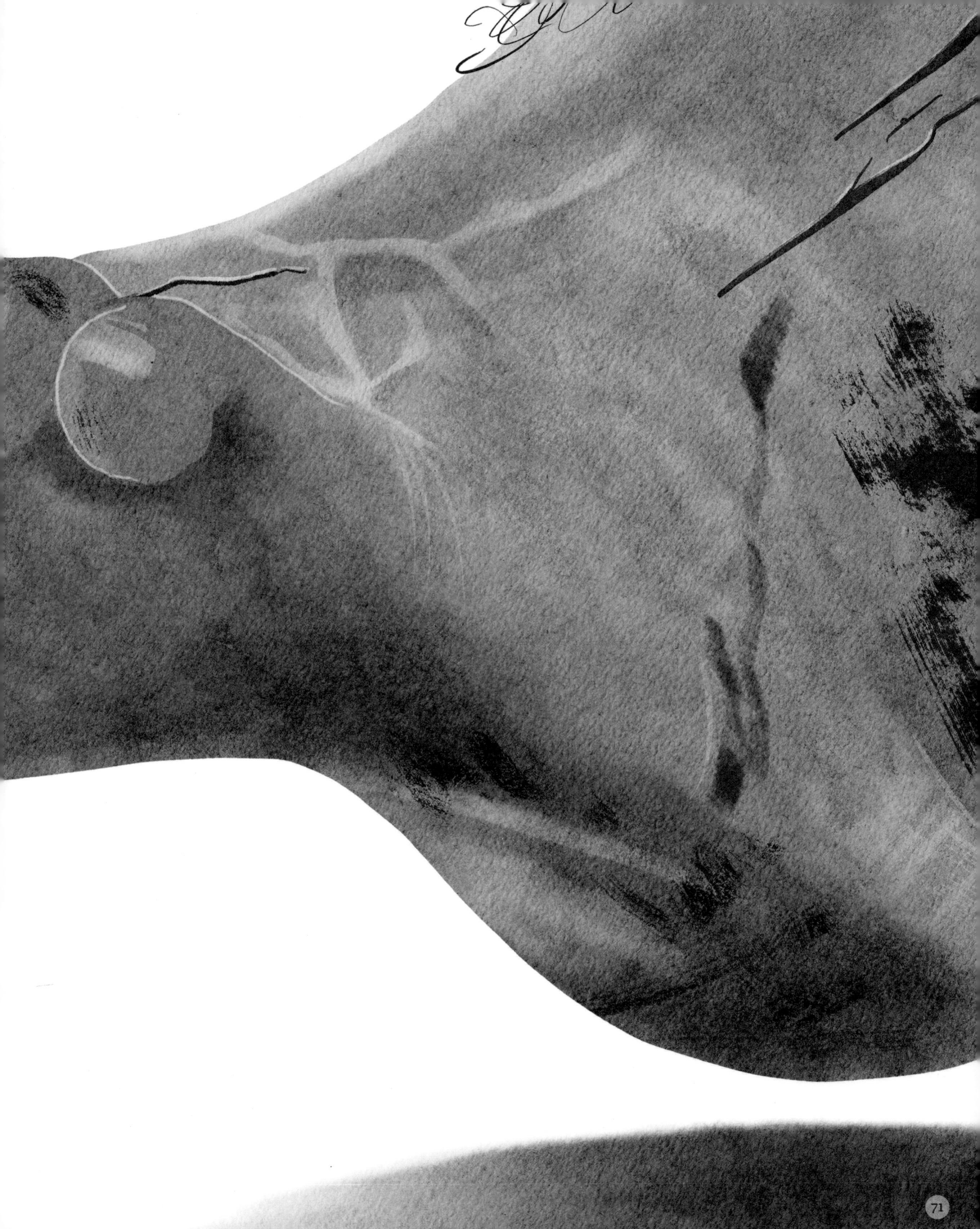

RETURN OF THE VICTORIA

There are only eighteen of them. The sole survivors of the 240 who initially set sail.

PORTUGAL
Vasco Gómez Gallego
Cabin boy

GREECE
Nicolás the Greek
Sailor

SPAIN
Juan Sebastián Elcano
Navigator / Captain

SPAIN
Antonio Hernández Colmenero
Sailor

PORTUGAL
Francisco Rodríguez
Sailor

ITALY
Martín de Judícibus
Merino (Judicial officer)

SPAIN
Diego Carmena Gallego
Sailor

SPAIN
Hernándo de Bustamante
Barber

GREECE
Francisco Albo
Pilot & Chronicler

SPAIN
Juan de Santander
Cabin boy

SPAIN
Juan de Acurio
Boatswain

SPAIN
Juan Rodríguez
Sailor

GREECE
Miguel de Rodas
Boatswain

SPAIN
Juan de Arratia
Cabin boy

GERMANY
Hans of Aachen
Gunner

GREECE
Miguel Sánchez
Sailor

ITALY
Antonio Pigafetta
Chronicler & Supernumerary

SPAIN
Juan de Zubileta
Squire

Three unnamed men from the Moluccas are also on board, having experienced a remarkable segment of this colossal journey.

BEYOND CLOVES

The completion of this journey is a triumph. Risking their lives, these sailors, like Enrique, have successfully circumnavigated the globe, providing evidence that the Earth is a sphere.

But the treasure these eighteen men have brought back is not the one they initially sought. It is neither the 381 sacks of cloves they have aboard – whose proceeds barely cover the expedition's costs – nor the title of being among the world's first circumnavigators.

Their view of the world has grown with each unknown path they have traversed. Here lies the true treasure: the awareness of the vastness of our world. The knowledge and experiences collected during their journey into the unknown. The perception of smells, sounds and flavours.

The diversity of every living thing they encountered. The opportunity to visit other places and engage with other cultures. Time has taught them how fleeting everything can be.

THE LEGACY

This voyage marked the dawn of an era that shaped the global world as we know it today. But, over the years, the tiny treasure at the beginning of it all has been overshadowed by the bigger details.

Cloves, and other spices, are a reminder not to overlook the smallest and most inconspicuous things – the things we take for granted. It is often in those things that significant history lies.

This great journey into the unknown reminds us that it's important to remain curious. History never belongs to one person alone. There is more than one way to tell it, and it depends on who you are listening to.

We might assume that we have learnt everything, but that is never true. Our world holds still more for us to understand or experience.

For each of us awaits a new, challenging, exciting journey into the unknown.

What will yours be?

GLOSSARY

archipelago (n.)
a group of islands that sit together in an ocean, lake or river

astronomical (adj.)
relating to the scientific study of the sun, the moon, the stars and the planets

baptise (v.)
when someone is baptised, they take part in a ceremony to become Christian and are splashed or covered with water

boatswain (n.)
the person on a ship whose job it is to take care of the equipment and the other people

Calicut (n.)
a city now known as Kozhikode

caravel (n.)
a small and fast sailing ship from Spain or Portugal around the fifteenth century

carrack (n.)
a European sailing ship with three or four masts from around the fourteenth century

Ceylon (n.)
an island now called Sri Lanka

Christian (n.)
someone who believes in the teachings of Jesus Christ, or the religion called Christianity

circumvent (v.)
to find a way around something

colonise (v.)
to take control of a place or country that is not yours, often using force, then send people from your country to live there; this process is called colonisation and described as colonial

continent (n.)
one of the seven main areas of land on earth: Asia, Africa, North America, South America, Antarctica, Europe and Oceania

culture (n.)
the customs, beliefs, artforms and ways of life shared by a group of people

Datu (n.)
a ruler from the Philippines islands

depose (v.)
to remove someone from their job post

enslave (v.)
to make one person the property of another; an enslaved person is forced to work for and obey someone else (note: sometimes the term 'slave' is used instead, but many prefer 'enslaved person' because it reminds us that slavery is forced onto someone and never a natural part of them)

equator (n.)
the imaginary line that goes round the centre of the Earth at an equal distance from the North Pole and the South Pole

flagship (n.)
the main ship in a fleet of ships

fleet (n.)
a group of ships commanded by one person

hunter-gatherer (n.)
a person who moves from place to place and gets food by hunting, fishing, and gathering plants

Indigenous (adj.)
relating to the people who come from a place and have lived there for longer than other people

maravedis (n.)
historical Spanish coins made of copper or gold

merchant (n.)
a person who buys and sells goods, often both within and outside of their own country

missionary (n.)
a person who goes to another country to teach people about religion, especially Christianity

mutiny (n.)
when a person or group of people (especially sailors or soldiers) refuse to obey the orders of someone in charge

nautical (adj.)
relating to ships, sailors and sailing

navigator (n.)
the person on a ship in charge of navigation, planning and directing where the ship will go

peninsula (n.)
a bit of land that is almost completely surrounded by water but remains joined to the mainland

provisions (n.)
supplies of food and drink

seafarer (n.)
a sailor

sovereignty (n.)
having total power over how a country is run

supernumerary (n.)
a passenger onboard a ship with no responsibilities or powers

uncharted (adj.)
not yet drawn on a map

For Irmi. – T.P.

My gratitude to all the places this project has taken me – from the islands of Sangihe, Ternate, Tidore and Ambon, to the museums in Seville, Lisbon and Sagres – and the treasures they hold. I am thankful to the many people I met along the way who generously shared their knowledge and insights. Last but not least, *beijos* to my friends and family.

The Voyage That Changed the World © 2025 Quarto Publishing plc. Text and Illustrations © 2025 Thekla Priebst

First Published in 2025 by Wide Eyed Editions,
an imprint of The Quarto Group.
1 Triptych Place, London, SE1 9SH, United Kingdom.
T (0)20 7700 6700 F (0)20 7700 8066 www.Quarto.com

The right of Thekla Priebst to be identified as the illustrator and author of this work has been asserted by them in accordance with the Copyright, Designs and Patents Act, 1988 (United Kingdom).

All rights reserved.

No part of this publication may be reproduced, stored in a retrieval system, or transmitted, in any form, or by any means, electrical, mechanical, photocopying, recording or otherwise without the prior written permission of the publisher or a licence permitting restricted copying.

A catalogue record for this book is available from the British Library.

ISBN 978-0-71129-347-2

The illustrations were created digitally
Set in Neue Kabel, Futura PT and Mala

Designer: Thekla Priebst and Sasha Moxon
Editor: Hannah Dove, Katie Taylor and Kimberley Davis
Consultants: Claire Sipi and Rue Dickey
Production Controller: Robin Boothroyd
Commissioning Editor: Hannah Dove
Art Director: Karissa Santos
Publisher: Debbie Foy

Manufactured in Johor, Malaysia CO062025

9 8 7 6 5 4 3 2 1